Effective Prayer
How to Pray Effectively

W. A. Contagious

Table of Contents

Introduction 4
Chapter 1: Prayer Is Our Effective Communication With God 5
Chapter 2: Prayer Makes Power Available 7
Chapter 3: Learn To Receive When You Pray 9
Chapter 4: The Prayer of a Righteous Man 11
Chapter 5: The Benefits of Praying In Tongues 13
Chapter 6: Learn To Pray Earnestly 15
Chapter 7: Prayer Produces Miracles 17
Chapter 8: The Prayer of Agreement 19
Chapter 9: The Prayer of Intercession 21
Chapter 10: Praying In The Name Of Jesus 23
Chapter 11: Be Constant In Prayer 25
Chapter 12: Learn To Prophesy In Prayer 27
Chapter 13: Pray With Knowledge 29
Chapter 14: Praise and Thanksgiving Prayers 31
Chapter 15: The Prayer of Faith 33
Chapter 16: Lifting Up Holy Hands in Prayer 35
Chapter 17: Prayer Conditions Your Spirit 37
Further Reading 39
About the Author 40

All scripture quotations are taken from the New King James and the Amplified Version, copyright ©1983 by Thomas Nelson, Inc. AV- Authorized Version of the Bible, crown copyright.

Introduction

Mathew 26:36

Then Jesus went with them to a place called Gethsemane, and He told His disciples, Sit down here while I go over yonder and pray.

The Greek word to pray is **proseuchomai** which means **to supplicate, worship, earnestly entreat, petition or implore.** It is an active spiritual exercise engaged in with earnestness, intensity, reverence, purpose and expectation. It is not something to be done with a beggarly, indifferent or irreverent attitude but in reverence and with earnest and intense determination to get results.

Prayer connotes an act of worship made to God; a superior authority and one who has the ability to bring to pass the subject of petition. It is also an earthly license for a heavenly interruption. If you cannot pray you cannot cause the heavens to respond to you. It is important to understand that God only answers prayed prayers, not wished prayers. Prayer produces power for results.

If you can kneel down before God in prayer, you can stand tall before any man. Prayerful men are powerful men. Prayer-less men are powerless men. Nothing works out until prayer is ignited. The greatest energy a man can generate is prayer energy. Do not worry about anything but instead pray about everything. You will experience peace which is far more wonderful than the human mind can understand. Every prayer time is an investment in eternity.

Chapter 1: Prayer Is Our Effective Communication With God

Luke 18:1

ALSO [Jesus] told them a parable to the effect that they ought always to pray and not to turn coward (faint, lose heart, and give up).

Communication is the most important activity in the lives of men. It is however encouraging to know that God also is a communicating God. He encourages us to communicate with him through prayer. Man is a spirit and his needs are spiritual, this is why he craves spiritual contact with God. It is therefore more than a blessing to note that you can communicate with God directly without interference and have his full attention in prayer.

1 Peter 3:16 *"For the eyes of the Lord are upon the righteous (those who are upright and in right standing with God), and His ears are attentive to their prayer. But the face of the Lord is against those who practice evil [to oppose them, to frustrate, and defeat them]."*

This is enough proof that God can be accessed through prayer with his attention focused on you. This is the reason why you always ought to pray. Some people pray only when they are in need. That should not be the case. The time of prayer is not only a time to ask God for things, but rather a time to commune or fellowship with him. It is a time to hear what he has to say and receive direction for each day's activity and challenges, and that is what Jesus used to do.

Mark 1:35 *"And in the morning, long before daylight, He got up and went out to a deserted place, and there He prayed."*

Jesus took prayer seriously while he was still on earth, because he understood the importance of communing with the Father. In one other occasion it is recorded that he prayed all night.

Luke 6:12 *"Now in those days it occurred that He went up into a mountain to pray, and spent the whole night in prayer to God."*

Though he was and is the Son of God, he did not take prayer for granted. He understood prayer. The moment you understand and embrace this truth, your life will become richer and you will be more productive in all your endeavors. You need that continuous fellowship with God to function effectively, otherwise, everything you do will be meaningless and will have no spiritual impact. Learn to rise up early to commune with the Lord. You should do this regularly.

Chapter 2: Prayer Makes Power Available
James 5:16

The earnest (heartfelt, continued) prayer of a righteous man makes tremendous power available [dynamic in its working].

The Greek word for power is translated as **"Dunamis" which means divine energy, might, strength for wonderful works, efficiency or miracle-working ability; it also means inherent dynamic ability to cause changes**. Therefore the earnest, heartfelt, continued prayer of the righteous man produces the dynamic ability to cause changes. It produces a miracle working ability.

Through prayer, you can produce the divine energy required to fix things in the realm of the spirit and effect the changes you desire in the physical as well. There is enough power in you to turn any situation around in your favour. You can change anything because divine might and power resides in you, it was deposited the moment you received the Holy Spirit in your life:

Acts 1:8 *"But you shall receive power (ability, efficiency, and might) when the Holy Spirit has come upon you.*

This power was made available to you the moment the Holy Spirit rested on you. However the presence of this power alone does not guarantee its availability. Just like you can be with someone, but be unavailable to the person. To be available means to be able to give your attention and cooperation in a matter.

Making tremendous power available only occurs when you set yourself apart to pray earnestly, fervently, passionately and intensively. You can watch yourself move from one level of glory to another and walk in the supernatural every day. Remember you carry in you a dynamic ability to cause changes and you can only unlock this power by praying earnestly for you to see every situation responding to this power.

Chapter 3: Learn To Receive When You Pray
Mathew 7:7-8

"Ask, and it shall be given you; seek, and ye shall find; knock, and it shall be opened unto you: For every one that asketh, receiveth; and he that seeketh, findeth; and to him that knocketh, it shall be opened."

It is amazing how a lot of people are busy praying, but many are too reluctant to receive. Most people are experts in praying, but amateurs in receiving. Praying without receiving is religion. Religion gives you nothing.

Many have learnt to pray earnestly but they have not learnt the faith way of receiving. Prayer is of no use if there is no receiving. Prayer was not meant to be a religious formality. Religion will compel you to pray as a rite and discourage you from looking forward to receiving answers to your prayers.

Religion can also make you see prayer only as an avenue to get God to do something for you. This can be frustrating when there are no answers. Jesus said we should always expect an answer.

Mark 11:24 *"For this reason I am telling you, whatever you ask for in prayer, believe (trust and be confident) that it is granted to you, and you will [get it].*

In other words when you pray, believe you have received and then you shall have whatsoever you have asked for. Every time you pray, God is busy answering. Therefore you also need to be busy receiving by faith.

How do you receive? Here is how you receive. Suppose you have prayed and asked the Lord for a particular thing. If you truly believe that your prayer has been answered, then you ought to declare immediately "glory to God, I have got what I have asked for" even if you may not be seeing it with your physical eyes. You need to act like you have already received it right from the moment you prayed for it.

That is how you receive when you pray. Jesus was very vivid in his communication through prayer to the Father. He realized that each time he prayed his Father was ready to grant his request. Learn the faith attitude to receive and prayer time will be a great time for you.

Chapter 4: The Prayer of a Righteous Man

Matthew 6:7

And when you pray, do not heap up phrases (multiply words, repeating the same ones over and over) as the unrighteous do, for they think they will be heard for their much speaking.

There is a difference in the way an unrighteous man prays and how a righteous man prays. The prayer of the righteous man is effectual, fervent and dynamic in its working. In other words, it produces genuine results.

God only delights in the prayers of the righteous man and not in the prayer of the unrighteous. The prayer of the unrighteous is ineffective and does not produce results. That is why Jesus urges us not to pray like they do, using vain repetitions and thinking that God will hear them through "much speaking". God does not hear or answer prayer because of the multiplicity of words. Sadly the perception of many people is the direct opposite.

Prayer is a spiritual exercise, and it is an act of faith. It has nothing to do with feelings or much speaking. You do not have to struggle in your prayer time for God to hear. Some people actually think that just because they are going through a tough season, then they need tough prayers. There is nothing like tough there is need to struggle in prayer intensely. It is the effectual fervent prayer of the righteous man that avails much and produces results, not the much speaking or strong prayer.

Every time you are praying, you need to pray the Word of God. That is how a righteous man prays, every time you pray realize the fact that you are the righteousness of God in Christ Jesus. All you need to do is to approach his throne of grace with boldness without any sense of guilt or condemnation knowing that the Lord delights in you and his pleasure is to answer your prayers.

Therefore avoid vain repetitions and pray the Word of God i.e. what God has promised in his Word. You must learn to pray the Word earnestly and fervently in faith just a like a righteous man and that is the prayer that works.

Chapter 5: The Benefits of Praying In Tongues

1 Corinthians 14:4

He who speaks in a [unknown] tongue edifies and improves himself.

Praying in super natural tongues is an effective spiritual way of communicating with God. Supernatural tongues or "other tongues" are a heavenly language that transcends the natural mind or intellect. When you pray in other tongues, you are stirred up in the "inner man".

The anointing wells up the currents within your spirit. This anointing impacts your physical body and rejuvenates you. It works on your mind such that you are able to pick up signals from the realms of the spirit and you are transported to the higher realms of glory. For you to experience spiritual growth, you need to pray or speak in supernatural tongues regularly. Every time you pray in tongues you build and edify yourself and ultimately improve yourself spiritually and physically.

Improving yourself is dependent on how much you value speaking in tongues. In fact the Bible says that we should strengthen our faith by praying in supernatural tongues.

Jude 1:20 *"But you, beloved, build yourselves up [founded] on your most holy faith [make progress, rise like an edifice higher and higher], praying in the Holy Spirit.*

When you pray in supernatural languages you are able to make spiritual progress and rise higher and higher. By speaking in tongues you embolden your spirit and you charge yourself up like a battery.

Praying in tongues is a tremendous blessing. It is not optional for a child of God. In fact it is improper for a child of God not to speak in tongues. If you want to be healthy spiritually, mentally and even physically, then you must pray in tongues often. One of the greatest secrets of the Apostle Paul for great success in his ministry was speaking in tongues.

1 Corinthians 14:18 *"I thank God that I speak in [unknown] tongues (languages) more than any of you or all of you put together.*

If you are born again and have received the Holy Spirit then you can and should pray in tongues as often as possible. You do not have to wait for special prayer times. Wherever you are, you can engage yourself in speaking in tongues and watch yourself grow tremendously and be refreshed.

Chapter 6: Learn To Pray Earnestly
James 5:16-17

The earnest (heartfelt, continued) prayer of a righteous man makes tremendous power available [dynamic in its working]. Elijah was a human being with a nature such as we have [with feelings, affections, and a constitution like ours]; and he prayed earnestly for it not to rain, and no rain fell on the earth for three years and six months.

To pray earnestly means to be intent and direct, zealous or fervent marked by a deep feeling of conviction. It means to be continuous with a feeling of the heart about a matter. It is the earnest prayer of a righteous man that produces results. Earnest prayer is a sustained kind of prayer that is marked by a deep feeling of conviction.

You do not just pray once and stop, but you continue seriously with a deep spirit of conviction until you get the note of victory in your spirit. Very few people pray this way, yet they expect to get the Elijah kind of results.

You need to learn to separate yourself and pray earnestly in private so that you can have the power of the Holy Spirit working for you in the public.

Before Elijah could proclaim to King Ahab that there would be no rain in the land, he had already talked to the Lord about it. He had prayed earnestly and continued in prayer until he got the answer.

Have you been earnest in your prayers? Do not give up until you achieve your desired objective for praying. Learn to pray earnestly, for it surely works. God has given you the ability to effect changes in and around you through your earnest, heartfelt, fervent and continued prayers. There is no situation that is too hopeless that you cannot change through prayer. Learn to pray earnestly.

Chapter 7: Prayer Produces Miracles

Proverbs 23:18

For surely there is a latter end [a future and a reward], and your hope and expectation shall not be cut off.

God's purpose for his children is for them to live in the realms of the supernatural all the days of their lives. Miracles are the acts of God. He demonstrates his love and closeness to us through the displays of the miraculous which are his supernatural manifestations in our lives.

How do you explain the fact that people are praying all over the world to a God they do not see and yet expect answers? Does this not show you the depths of man's desire to communicate with the supernatural?

Think about it. Every answered prayer is a miracle. It does not matter what it was that you prayed for. The fact that you received an answer indicates it was a miracle. God in his sovereignty will even perform a miracle for you when you are not expecting it at all. Is this not amazing? He shows up on your behalf because of his love for you. So every time you pray expect a miracle, because God is a miracle working God. He is not a magician, but he is God.

A lot of people claim to love God but do not believe in miracles, in fact they preach against it. Then what is the essence of praying if there are no answers to your prayers?

Because every answered prayer is a miracle, a miracle is the intervention of God to do for you what you could not do for yourself. If any man could do it for you, then there would be no business disturbing God with your prayers. The fact that you consulted him through prayer and he answered you is adequate proof that it was a miracle.

Every time you pray, expect a miracle. It is simply a religious attitude for you to pray and not expect answers. Your expectation for answers is what I call faith, and when God answers, then it becomes a miracle. Expect a miracle today. Your prayers have been answered. Wait for your miracle.

Chapter 8: The Prayer of Agreement

Matthew 18:19-20

Again I tell you, if two of you on earth agree (harmonize together, make a symphony together) about whatever [anything and everything] they may ask, it will come to pass and be done for them by My Father in heaven.

The Greek word for agree is translated as *sumphoneo* which means to be harmonious, to concur, to accord and to stipulate by compact.

Therefore an agreement is an accord, a concord, an understanding between two or more people or groups of people. It is a harmony or meeting of thoughts, ideas and reason. In other words two or more believers can consent, that is come to a mutual agreement on any situation that they want changed and then through prayer, which is the prayer of agreement, that change is effected.

The prayer of agreement is one way we can bring to pass what we desire and effect changes in and around us with God's Word. So in the prayer of agreement, there is concord and accord between the parties involved. The purpose for the prayer is clearly spelt out, and the request is made in faith and in line with the word of God. Having done all that, then you can be certain that your prayers would be answered. The Bible says:

1 John 5:14 *"And this is the confidence (the assurance, the privilege of boldness) which we have in Him: [we are sure] that if we ask anything (make any request) according to His* *wiil (in agreement with His own plan), He listens to and hears us.*

The next time you want to effect a change in any situation, follow the rules of the prayer of agreement. It is a sure way of praying and getting results.

Chapter 9: The Prayer of Intercession

Jeremiah 27:18

"But if they are true prophets and if the word of the Lord is really spoken by them, let them now make intercession to the Lord of hosts that the vessels which are [still] left in the house of the Lord, in the house of the king of Judah, and in Jerusalem may not go to Babylon."

There is an intercessory ministry of the Holy Spirit which He carries out through the believer, but there is also the intercessory ministry of the believer, and the two are different.

The Holy Spirit carries out his intercessory ministry through us. You may be led by God to pray for someone or minister to them by the leading of the Holy Spirit. You may even be praying for other things and suddenly the Spirit of God begins to work within you and you find yourself praying for what you did not plan for. By the leading of God's Spirit, you just find yourself heading towards that direction.

However you do not always have to wait for that prompting before you pray for others. Our intercessory ministry as believers requires us to pray for others, without even the leading of the spirit. It is something you do consciously, when you intercede for others in accordance with God's word. God will hear you just as if the Holy Spirit had inspired you to pray for that particular scenario. There are however certain rules that govern intercessory prayer which must be taken into consideration.

First you must know that you are not interceding for yourself. The prayer of intercession is always on behalf of someone else. Secondly, you need to be persistent about whatever it is that you are interceding for. This is because you are trying to prevail on someone else to align with God's will.

In the prayer of intercession, you are concentrating the influence of God's power on others for their good, and that requires some persistence in prayer. Not only must you be persistent, you must also continue in prayer for as long as it takes for it to work. In the prayer of intercession, you do not stop praying until you get the note of victory in your spirit and are certain that you have got what you have asked for.

You need to understand that the ministry of intercession has been committed to you. All you have to do is to be consistent and persistent while concentrating in your intercessory prayer and you will see the influence of God's power over the people you are interceding for.

Chapter 10: Praying In The Name Of Jesus
John 16:23

And when that time comes, you will ask nothing of Me [you will need to ask Me no questions]. I assure you, most solemnly I tell you, that My Father will grant you whatever you ask in My Name [as presenting all that I AM].

Up to this time you have not asked a [single] thing in My Name [as presenting all that I AM]; but now ask and keep on asking and you will receive, so that your joy (gladness, delight) may be full and complete.

All through scripture, there is no place where a believer is permitted to pray to Jesus or through Jesus, but rather it teaches us to pray in the name of Jesus. That is the only right way to pray. Unfortunately this mystery has been hidden to many.

You therefore find people praying the wrong way, like someone says; "Lord Jesus, I ask that you grant me such and such in Jesus name" no this is wrong prayer, you do not pray to Jesus in the name of Jesus, neither do you pray to the Father through the name of Jesus, but you pray to the Father in the name of Jesus. This is the right way to pray.

You may fellowship with Jesus, and tell him how much you love him, but you do not pray to him, but rather to the Father in the name of Jesus for any request to be granted. You need to realize that as a Christian, you do not need an intermediary between you and the Father, therefore to pray through Jesus is to make him your medium or intermediary to the Father which should not be the case, but to pray in the name of Jesus means you are standing in the place of Jesus.

You have become his voice, in other words, even you are the one asking the Father for something. Jesus is actually the one asking him, this is why it is impossible for God not to grant your requests when you ask by faith in the name of Jesus. Jesus has given us the legal right to use his name.

We have the power of attorney to function in his stead, just like a delegated member of a president's cabinet can represent him at a state function. When that person arrives at the function, he will perform all necessary protocols in the name of the president, since he is there in the president's stead. In the same way, you are in the place of Jesus, so you cannot pray through him anymore, he has delegated his authority to you. All you have to do is to pray in his name, and get results.

Chapter 11: Be Constant In Prayer

Romans 12:11-12

Never lag in zeal and in earnest endeavor; be aglow and burning with the Spirit, serving the Lord. Rejoice and exult in hope; be steadfast and patient in suffering and tribulation; be constant in prayer.

A lot of people think that prayer is about telling God your problems and hoping that He will do something about them. That is a wrong perception on the subject of prayer. Prayer is two-way traffic. It is a fellowship or communion with your heavenly Father. You are not just talking to him, but with him and he talks to you as well.

Therefore constant communion with him helps to build your relationship with your heavenly Father. For you to grow and strengthen your love with God, you have to learn to be consistent in prayer and make prayer a part of your daily routine. Some people only pray when things are out of control, because they have a wrong perception of prayer.

They think that prayer is all about getting God to fix things quickly for you and that is it. Amazingly that is not how it works. There is a transformation that takes place in your life every time you spend more time to commune with God in prayer.

Your character and thoughts are continuously influenced by the presence of God, and you find yourself becoming like him. You begin to talk his language and reason like him. Then you are transported to a higher realm of the supernatural where nothing is impossible to you.

Prayer is guaranteed to change your life, if you do it consistently. That is why we are admonished to be constant in our prayers even in the presence of tribulations and hard times.

Chapter 12: Learn To Prophesy In Prayer
1 Corinthians 14:1

Eagerly pursue and seek to acquire [this] love [make it your aim, your great quest]; and earnestly desire and cultivate the spiritual endowments (gifts), especially that you may prophesy (interpret the divine will and purpose in inspired preaching and teaching).

The Greek for prophesy is translated as *propheteuo* which means to foretell events divinely and to speak under an inspiration of the Holy Spirit to prophesy therefore is to speak forth the word of God in power, whether by foretelling of future events or as a rhema-word to cause a change in the now. The Bible says:

1 Corinthians 14:3-4 *"But [on the other hand], the one who prophesies [who interprets the divine will and purpose in inspired preaching and teaching] speaks to men for their up building and constructive spiritual progress and encouragement and consolation. He who speaks in a [strange] tongue edifies and improves himself, but he who prophesies [interpreting the divine will and purpose and teaching with inspiration] edifies and improves the church and promotes growth [in Christian wisdom, piety, holiness, and happiness].*

Every time you declare the mind of God in prophecy, others are edified, strengthened and comforted hence constructive spiritual progress is ignited. Every time the mind of God is spoken out, the church is improved and growth is enhanced.

It is therefore the will of God that you have the gift of prophecy, but it begins with your desire for it. This gift is not only for a special few. It is not only for preachers or for church elders. It is for the church. God wants you to have this gift of prophecy. Start to desire it if you do not have it, and before long, it will be a part of you.

Moses in the Old Testament understood the power and the importance of prophecy and he wished that all of God's children prophesied:

Numbers 11:29 *"But Moses said to him: Are you envious or jealous for my sake? Would that the entire Lord's people were prophets and that the Lord would put His Spirit upon them!"*

We thank God we are now born-again and have received the Spirit of God. The divine enablement and the inspiration to prophesy, consequently, whether you are praying on your own or in the company of other believers, you can prophesy, as the Word of God wells up in you under the influence of the Holy Spirit. Open your mouth and speak forth those words in prophesy without fear.

If you have never prophesied, begin to desire the gift of prophecy, because the manifestation of the Spirit was given to every man. This means you too can prophesy. As you begin to prophesy, the Spirit will fill your mouth with words of power to cause changes around you and other people as you declare his word of Glory.

Your future will be a success. Progress and prosperity will accompany you daily. Grace and favor will follow you all the days of your life. You will begin to experience peace and divine health, as you experience joy and goodness on every side of your life.

Chapter 13: Pray With Knowledge

1 John 5:14

And this is the confidence (the assurance, the privilege of boldness) which we have in Him: [we are sure] that if we ask anything (make any request) according to His will (in agreement with His own plan), He listens to and hears us.

Knowledge means *the fact or condition of knowing something with familiarity gained through experience or association*. It also means *acquaintance with or understanding of a science, art or technique. It is the fact or condition of being aware of something*. Other synonyms of knowledge are cognition, erudition, learning and scholarship.

There are a couple of Greek words that denote Knowledge in the New Testament. One of them is **gnosis** which means *scientific or empirical knowledge*, which is akin to the definitions above. Another translation is **epignosis** which refers to *revelation knowledge, knowledge by discernment, knowledge with participation*. It makes you understand how to apply what you know and have received, and the power behind that revelation. *Epignosis* is the highest kind of revelation knowledge.

With this kind of knowledge, the immeasurable blessings and provisions of God become a vital reality in your life. When you have knowledge about them and you begin to proclaim them in prayer. It is important to pray, but praying would not be effective if you do not know the word of God.

If you are not properly grounded in God's Word, you will only know how to pray religious prayers borne out of unbelief.

Praying without knowledge is the reason for unanswered prayers.

The Bible says in **Proverbs 19:11**

"But through knowledge and superior discernment shall the righteous be delivered".

Your prayer only becomes effective in the realm of the spirit when knowledge is applied. Watch this; I am not talking about head knowledge or the knowledge of arts and sciences. I am referring to the knowledge of God's Word. Praying according to the Word of God is the prayer that works; not just any prayer. You see anybody can pray, but not everybody receives answers to their prayers. The fact that you have prayed does not necessarily mean that God answered you. God only answers prayers that are prayed in accordance with his will. His will is revealed in his Word.

Therefore begin to learn to pray in accordance to the knowledge of God's Word, and you will see God hearing and answering your prayers.

Chapter 14: Praise and Thanksgiving Prayers

Philippians 4:6

Do not fret or have any anxiety about anything, but in every circumstance and in everything, by prayer and petition (definite requests), with thanksgiving, continue to make your wants known to God.

1 Peter 2:5

[Come] and, like living stones, be yourselves built [into] a spiritual house, for a holy (dedicated, consecrated) priesthood, to offer up [those] spiritual sacrifices [that are] acceptable and pleasing to God through Jesus Christ.

Praise is an act of expression in speech of approval, admiration or honor. Thus praising God is the act of giving him thanks for definite reasons. Our responsibility in this new dispensation of grace demands that we give God praise, just as the priests in the Old Testament who offered sacrifices and burnt offerings as a sign of praise and thanksgiving to God.

We too have to praise and thank him through our words, presenting our bodies to him and living holy lives before him. These are our expressions of worship.

The sacrifices of praise that we should offer include are our confessions, declarations, psalms, hymns and spiritual songs of glory, grace, and goodness of God that we make unto him. As we do this, we send forth incense unto God. It is impossible for a sinner to do this.

Anybody can pray, but it takes a child of God to send forth incense by the spirit into the presence of God. As you learn to worship and praise God, prayer becomes interesting and enjoyable rather than a nightmare.

Chapter 15: The Prayer of Faith
Mark 11:22-23

And Jesus answering saith unto them, have faith in God. For verily I say unto you, that whosoever shall say unto this mountain, be thou removed, and be thou cast into the sea; and shall not doubt in his heart, but shall believe that those things which he saith shall come to pass; he shall have whatsoever he saith.

The prayer of faith is one of the different kinds of prayer. It has its peculiar rules and requirements. This kind of prayer involves making a request to God and speaking to circumstances without having any doubt in your heart. To have faith in God means to have the God kind of faith, the supernatural faith that God applies. The word believe in the above scripture is formed from two Anglo-Saxon words. The first word means *to accept that something exists*, and the second word means *to act like it.*

Thus making the word believe an action word that brings about possession. The believer therefore is a possessor, not one only living in the realm of hope. You cannot afford to only live in the realm of hope. Begin to possess. The Bible also says *"whosoever shall say unto this mountain..."*. This means anything is possible by your declaration of faith. As you issue commands in faith without doubting, you will have whatever you say. Is this not amazing?

The prayer of faith is prayed for the things that concern you or are under your authority. In this prayer of faith, there must be a specific desire, a faith utterance, a definite belief in your heart that gives no place for doubt, and the assurance that what you say must surely come to pass.

As you begin to pray with this kind of understanding, your life will begin to take an upward and forward momentum that is irreversible, because God's word has the ability to produce for you what you confess in prayer. Begin to speak forth your word with faith in your spirit, as you speak, and believe that those things that you say will come to pass. You will have whatever you say. Go for it. It works and it will always work. Begin to speak in accordance with the Word of God and see your life gaining shape.

Chapter 16: Lifting Up Holy Hands in Prayer

1 Timothy 2:8

I desire therefore that in every place men should pray, without anger or quarreling or resentment or doubt [in their minds], lifting up holy hands.

Lifting up of holy hands to God during prayer and worship is a deep revelation that has been hidden from many today. Many do not know the importance of this holy act. One of the generals of God who understood this holy act was David. Much as he lived in the Old Testament times he had a New Testament revelation. Look at what he says:

Psalms 141:2 *"Let my prayer be set forth as incense before You, the lifting up of my hands as the evening sacrifice."*

This is what true worship in prayer is. Lifting up of holy hands to God during prayer and worship is far more pleasing to him than the offering of a physical sacrifice.

Therefore if the Lord delights in the lifting up of holy hands, then you ought to take it seriously. It has nothing to do with whether or not you feel like lifting up your holy hands to him. You just ought to do it. It is a training you imbibe, for it is a spiritual act of obedience. Provided you are born-again, you have holy hands.

Hebrews 3:1 *"Wherefore, holy brethren, partakers of the heavenly calling, consider the Apostle and High Priest of our profession, Christ Jesus".*

This is proof that you are holy. Therefore your hands too are holy. Hence practice how to lift your holy hands to God during worship and prayer, and you will be ignited with the presence of God like never before as you also tap in to the anointing of the Spirit. Why not begin to practice this now, and see God's presence manifest upon your life?

Chapter 17: Prayer Conditions Your Spirit
Ephesians 6:18

Pray at all times (on every occasion, in every season) in the Spirit, with all [manner of] prayer and entreaty. To that end keep alert and watch with strong purpose and perseverance, interceding in behalf of all the saints (God's consecrated people).

The most exciting thing about prayer is the impact it has on your human spirit. Many people pray because of their needs that have to be met by God. However, there is more to prayer than just asking him to fix your needs. Prayer is a time of worship and fellowship.

This is where praying in the spirit plays a big role in conditioning your spirit as a result enhancing sensitivity to the realities of the kingdom of God. You need to understand that you do not pray so that God can do anything for you. He has already done all that is necessary. He has already given you all things!

Prayer therefore, amongst its other benefits, conditions your spirit to receive. Jesus always prayed, but he prayed because of what prayer did to his spirit. Every time he came down from the mountain after prayer, tremendous miracles followed, because his spirit had been stirred with the power of God. This is one beautiful reason as to why you should pray in other tongues profusely for the conditioning of your spirit. It makes it easy for you to receive spiritual guidance.

A lot of people who go astray and fall in the devils trap do so because their spirits are not conditioned so as to receive divine guidance.

As you begin this journey today of conditioning your spirit by praying in other tongues, you will receive divine thoughts, ideas and counsel in your spirit. As you fellowship with the Spirit of God, divine impartation and transformation will begin to take place in your life.

Further Reading

FAITH WORLD MEDIA
PRODUCTS

- How to recreate your world by the Word
- How to recreate your world by faith
- How to recreate your world with your words
- Who is the Holy Spirit
- Your rights in Christ
- Working the Word
- The Concept of Righteousness
- How to work your faith

About the Author

To Contact The Author:
In Kenya: *Write to*

W. A. Contagious
Believers Faith World Inc. aka Miracle Embassy
P.O. Box 219-00204 Nairobi-Kenya
Phone: +254-700.521542

In Uganda: *Write to*

W. A. Contagious
Believers Faith World Inc. aka Miracle Embassy
P.O. Box 1987 Kampala-Uganda
Phone: +256-712.191525

Email: contagiousw@hotmail.com

www.ingramcontent.com/pod-product-compliance
Lightning Source LLC
LaVergne TN
LVHW021743060526
838200LV00052B/3434